Military
HORSES

by Michael Sandler

Consultant: Randall E. Davis, Jr.
Captain, Transportation Corps
U.S. Army

BEARPORT
PUBLISHING

New York, New York

Credits

Cover and Title Page, © Joseph Sohm; ChromoSohm Inc./Corbis; 4, © Mary Evans Picture Library/ Alamy; 5, © North Wind Picture Archives/Northwind; 6, © HIP/Art Resource, NY; 7, © AP Images/ Daniel Hulshizer; 8, © The Art Archive; 9, © Juniors Bildarchiv/Alamy; 10, © The Granger Collection, New York; 11, © Erich Lessing/Art Resource, NY; 12, © North Wind Picture Archives/Northwind; 13, © Mark J. Barrett/Alamy; 14, © EASTCOTT/MOMATIUK/Animals Animals Earth Scenes; 15, © CORBIS; 16, © The Art Archive/National Archives Washington DC; 17, © Bettmann/Corbis; 18, © Newberry Library, Chicago, Illinois, USA/The Bridgeman Art Library; 19, © Bildarchiv Preussischer Kulturbesitz/Art Resource, NY; 20, © Private Collection/Peter Newark American Pictures/The Bridgeman Art Library; 21, © Mark J. Barrett/Alamy; 22, © CORBIS; 23, © Australian War Memorial; 24, © US Cavalry Museum, Fort Riley, Kansas; 25, Photo Courtesy Col. Edwin Ramsey, www. EdwinPriceRamsey.com; 26, © Chris McGrath/Getty Images/NewsCom.com; 27, © Spencer Platt/ Getty Images/NewsCom.com; 28, © Eric J. Enger/Shutterstock; 29TR, © Robert Maier/Animals Animals Earth Scenes; 29TL, © Bob Langrish; 29M, © Robert Maier/Animals Animals Earth Scenes; 29BL, © Eline Spek/Shutterstock; 29BR, © Dominique Braud/Animals Animals Earth Scenes.

Publisher: Kenn Goin
Project Editor: Lisa Wiseman
Creative Director: Spencer Brinker
Photo Researcher: Jennifer Bright
Design: Stacey May

Library of Congress Cataloging-in-Publication Data

Sandler, Michael.
 Military horses / by Michael Sandler.
    p. cm. — (Horse power)
 Includes bibliographical references and index.
 ISBN-13: 978-1-59716-402-3 (library binding)
 ISBN-10: 1-59716-402-X (library binding)
 1. War horses—Juvenile literature. I. Title.

 UE460.S35 2007
 357'.1—dc22

                    2006036300

For more information, write to Bearport Publishing Company, Inc., 101 Fifth Avenue, Suite 6R, New York, New York 10003. Printed in the United States of America.

10 9 8 7 6 5 4 3 2 1

Contents

A Boy and His Horse

Alexander and his father looked at the black **stallion**. "He's too wild, too strong," said his father. "No one can ride him."

"I can," replied Alexander. His father was amazed as the boy calmly climbed onto the **headstrong** animal named Bucephalus (*boo*-SEF-uh-luhss).

A young Alexander taming Bucephalus

Around 336 B.C., Alexander became a very powerful ruler. His armies conquered Europe and Asia. A **cavalry** was his most dangerous weapon. His soldiers on horseback swung their swords as they **galloped** through enemy lines. Alexander always rode Bucephalus, the powerful warhorse he had tamed as a child.

Alexander and his army in battle

Bucephalus died a hero at age 30. Right before his death, Bucephalus was wounded. Still, he was able to save Alexander's life by carrying him off the battlefield.

Weapons of War

For thousands of years, horses have carried soldiers into war. The very first military horses charged onto the battlefield in about 2000 B.C. These animals pulled **chariots** as soldiers fired arrows or spears at the enemy.

Ramses II, an Egyptian pharaoh, aims his arrow at the enemy while guiding his chariot.

Before using horses in war, humans needed a way to control them. The invention of the **bit** helped people manage these animals.

Chariots gave soldiers a huge advantage against those who didn't have them. The sight of the speeding carts and the roar of thundering hooves was often enough to win a battle. Scared enemy soldiers on foot often turned and ran way. This way of fighting was so successful that soon the ancient Romans and Egyptians added chariots to their armies.

The Egyptians and Romans also used their chariots for racing. A form of that sport, harness racing, still exists today.

Soldiers on Horseback

Early horses were too small and weak to support a person's weight. So people began **breeding** larger ones with stronger muscles. Soon riding on top of a horse became possible. By around 1000 B.C., soldiers began fighting on horseback.

A female Japanese warrior on horseback

Trousers were most likely invented to protect the legs of horse riders. In 1000 B.C., **mounted** soldiers were among the very first to wear these pants.

These soldiers were more successful than those riding in chariots. Chariots could roll only across flat dry ground. At high speeds, they often tipped over. Mounted soldiers were faster than chariots and could do much more. On horseback, soldiers easily climbed hills, passed through forests, and crossed rivers. They were able to quickly cover lots of ground to gather information about the enemy.

The Akhal-Teke is one of the world's oldest breeds of horses.

Warriors of Asia

Many different **breeds** of horses were used for military work. The Huns, fierce warriors of central Asia, rode small shaggy ponies. Carrying little armor and using light weapons, these soldiers didn't need bigger animals. Their **agile** horses could handle the toughest mountain **terrain**. They could also travel for very long distances.

Attila was the cruel and powerful king of the Huns around 434 A.D. Here he leads his warriors into Italy.

Huge groups of Huns would fire blizzards of arrows as they swooped down on their enemies. They were able to carry out these attacks because they were among the first to use **stirrups**. This equipment allowed soldiers to brace themselves against the horses. They could then shoot arrows without falling off the animals.

The Great Wall of China is the longest structure ever built. It's about 4,500 miles (7,242 km) long and was made completely by hand.

China began work on its famous Great Wall to keep out the Huns and their horses!

Knights of Europe

In Europe, during **medieval** times (400s–1400s A.D.), there was a new kind of mounted soldier—the knight. For protection, these soldiers wore heavy armor that could be 400 pounds (181 kg) or more.

Since they weighed so much, knights needed very strong horses to carry them. Some of the world's biggest horses, such as the English Shire and the French Percheron, were bred just for these soldiers.

Often, a knight's horse wore armor, too.

Falling off a horse was often deadly for a knight. Unable to move quickly in his armor, the soldier became easy **prey** for his enemies.

During battle, two lines of knights galloped toward each other. They tried to gather enough power to knock each other off their horses with their weapons.

Even though these bulky warhorses could carry the heavy knights, they weren't very fast. They could go only about 15 miles per hour (24 kph).

Though Percherons are strong horses, they are also known as gentle, steady animals.

Military Horses from Spain

In 1519, Hernando Cortés from Spain landed on the Mexican coast. The Native American people who met him were amazed. They stared at the huge Spanish ships. They jumped at the sound of Spanish guns. Most of all, however, they looked in awe at the horses. Never before had they seen animals like these. In North America, horses had been **extinct** for 10,000 years.

This Mustang is related to the horses brought to North America by Cortés.

Military horses helped Cortés conquer the great empire of the **Aztecs**. Some horses were set loose. They spread across the land. Native Americans began using them for hunting and transportation. Like the Spanish, they also began using them for war.

Native Americans on horseback

The freed Spanish horses became known as American Mustangs. Today, there are more than 40,000 of them living in the western United States.

Training for War

In the autumn of 1861, the Civil War (1861–1865) was underway. At Camp Scott in Staten Island, New York, young soldiers reported for duty.

Soon, they would fight as the 6th New York Cavalry. First, however, **Union** Colonel Thomas Devin had to train his new soldiers. They learned to pack a saddle and how to care for a horse. They studied mounting, dismounting, and riding together in units. They practiced using **sabers** and guns on horseback.

Colonel Devin (right, standing) and some Union generals plan their attack.

The horses also needed training. Instructors banged drums, waved flags, and even fired guns in front of them. They needed to learn to not be afraid of the sights and sounds of war.

The Battle of Gettysburg

The 6th New York Cavalry served in dozens of battles. They fought at the Battle of Gettysburg, a turning point of the Civil War.

The Dangers of War

Life for military horses was sometimes short. Battle wounds weren't their only danger. Thirst and **starvation** killed many. Others died from disease or infection. Often, no medical care was available. During the Civil War, many cavalry horses survived for only six months.

More horses died in the North than in the South during the Civil War. Why? The Southerners knew how to take better care of their animals.

Sometimes, horses were even killed by their riders. Years before the Civil War, French general Napoleon Bonaparte launched an invasion of Russia in 1812. He was forced to retreat when the brutal winter set in. His soldiers, freezing and without supplies, began to starve. The poor horses that had survived many battles were killed and eaten by the hungry men.

Napoleon's men and horses battle the brutal winter in Russia.

Around 200,000 horses died during Napoleon's attack on Russia.

Comanche

Sometimes, however, the horses fared better than their riders. On June 25, 1876, Myles Keogh rode into battle on a horse named Comanche. Keogh, a U.S. cavalry soldier, was fighting under the command of General George Custer.

Comanche

Custer's troops were trying to force Sioux and Cheyenne Indians to move onto **reservations**. These Native Americans were fighting to keep their land and way of life.

Though the Native Americans would lose this war, on this day they won the battle. By the end, Keogh, Custer, and every other soldier lay dead. The only survivor was Comanche!

The Sioux Indians rode Bashkir Curly horses. This breed has slightly wavy hair on their tails and manes.

After the battle, Comanche was never ridden again. He was allowed to retire.

A New Kind of War

In the 1900s, the importance of military horses began to lessen. New weapons and vehicles made fighting on horseback impossible. Mounted soldiers stood little chance against machine guns, bombs, and tanks.

With the use of tanks, soldiers didn't need to ride on horseback to reach the enemy.

Even without military horses, the term *cavalry* continues to be used. Today, the title refers to army units with tanks.

During World War I (1914–1918), however, millions of horses were still able to serve the military in many other ways. They dragged cannons into firing position, pulled ambulances to the battlefield, and brought supplies to troops.

By World War II (1939–1945), however, even these jobs were taken over by jeeps and trucks. There were very few times that military horses rode into battle.

During World War I, pulling ambulances was an important job for military horses.

The Last Cavalry Charge

The U.S. Army's final cavalry charge took place on January 16, 1942, in the Philippines. There, U.S. and **Filipino** soldiers were fighting together against **invading** Japanese troops during World War II.

Lieutenant Ed Ramsey of the 26th Cavalry got his orders. He and his troops were to take over the town of Morong.

The 26th Cavalry in the Philippines

Once there, they were attacked by Japanese soldiers who carried machine guns. Ramsey decided to let his skilled horsemen do what they did best.

"I brought up my arm and yelled to my men to charge," said Ramsey. At a fast gallop with guns out, the soldiers drove the Japanese away from Morong.

Lieutenant Ed Ramsey on his horse, Brynn Awryn

After World War II, Ramsey would be awarded 16 American and Philippine awards and medals.

Military Horses Today

Today, horses no longer dodge bullets or charge at enemy troops. Still, the **tradition** of the military horse lives on.

In the Olympic sport of dressage, skills that once served the needs of generals now earn gold medals for the winning riders. In a series of tests, riders show off their horses' strength and agility.

Jan Brink, of Sweden, rides his horse, Briar, during a dressage event in the 2004 Summer Olympics in Athens, Greece.

The tradition is also seen at military funerals. As the body of a **veteran** is carried to his grave, a riderless horse follows the **casket**. In the horse's stirrups is a pair of empty boots. These symbolize the loss of the soldier.

Though military horses now have different roles than in the past, there is one thing that will always remain the same. These amazing animals will always be heroes.

A riderless horse trails the casket at the funeral of President Ronald Reagan in 2004.

When a U.S. President dies, a riderless horse also takes part in the funeral **procession**.

Just the Facts

- U.S. Special Forces parachuted into Afghanistan to fight the **Taliban** in 2001. In many places the land was too rugged for jeeps. So the troops got around the same way soldiers did hundreds of years ago. They rode small Afghan ponies on the winding mountain trails. During the war, horses also helped haul equipment. They played an important role in the Taliban's loss.

- Most horses live about 20 years. Horses usually retire from military service when they are about 15 years old.

- The tallest horse on record was a Percheron named Dr. Le Gear. This animal stood 7 feet tall (2 m) and weighed 3,020 pounds (1,370 kg).

- The last U.S. cavalry horse, Chief, entered service in 1941. He died 27 years later. He was buried with full military honors.

Common Breeds

Military Horses

Shire

Percheron

Mongolian

Arabian

Mustang

Glossary

agile (AJ-il) able to move around easily and gracefully

Aztecs (AZ-teks) people of a Native American empire in Mexico, during the 1400s through the early 1500s

bit (BIT) the metal bar that goes into a horse's mouth and is attached to the reins

breeding (BREED-ing) the process of keeping animals with special characteristics so that they can mate and produce offspring with those same characteristics

breeds (BREEDZ) types of horses

casket (KASS-kit) a wooden or metal container that a dead person is buried in

cavalry (KAH-vuhl-ree) soldiers who ride on horseback

chariots (CHA-ree-uhts) small carts that are pulled by horses

extinct (ek-STINGKT) when an animal or plant species dies out

Filipino (fil-a-PEE-noh) a person who is from the Philippines

galloped (GAL-uhpt) horses running at the fastest pace

headstrong (HED-strawng) bold, hard to control

invading (in-VAYD-ing) trying to take over an area

medieval (meh-DEE-vuhl) from the time of the Middle Ages, around the 400s through the 1400s A.D.

mounted (MOUNT-id) on horseback

prey (PRAY) someone who is helpless or unable to fight back

procession (pruh-SESH-uhn) a group of people walking or driving along a route as part of a parade or religious service

reservations (*rez*-ur-VAY-shuhnz) land set aside by the government for a special purpose

sabers (SAY-berz) curved swords

stallion (STAL-yuhn) a male horse

starvation (star-VAY-shuhn) to suffer or die from hunger

stirrups (STIR-ups) metal rings that hang from a horse's saddle used to support a rider's feet

Taliban (TAL-ah-ban) a military and political group who ruled Afghanistan from 1996 to 2001

terrain (tuh-RAYN) type of land

tradition (truh-DISH-uhn) a belief, idea, or custom that is handed down from generation to generation

trousers (TROU-zurz) clothing that covers the lower half of a person's body; pants

Union (YOON-yuhn) the Northern side in the American Civil War

veteran (VET-ur-uhn) a person who has served in the military

Bibliography

Ambrus, Victor G. *Horses in Battle*. London: Oxford University Press (1975).

Glueckstein, Fred. "The Last Mounted Cavalry Charge: Luzon 1942." *Army Magazine*, July 2005.

Jurmain, Suzanne. *Once Upon a Horse: A History of Horses— And How They Shaped Our History*. New York: HarperCollins (1989).

Lawrence, Elizabeth Atwood. *His Very Silence Speaks: Comanche—The Horse Who Survived Custer's Last Stand*. Detroit, MI: Wayne State University Press (1989).

Read More

Felber, Bill. *The Horse in War*. Philadelphia: Chelsea House Publishers (2002).

Gaff, Jackie. *Alexander the Great*. Columbus, OH: Peter Bedrick (2003).

Garland, Sherry. *The Buffalo Soldier*. Gretna, LA: Pelican (2006).

Nobleman, Marc Tyler. *The Battle of Little Big Horn*. Minneapolis, MN: Compass Point Books (2001).

Learn More Online

To learn more about military horses, visit
www.bearportpublishing.com/HorsePower

Index

About the Author

Michael Sandler has written numerous books for kids and young adults. He lives in Brooklyn, New York, with fellow writer Sunita Apte and their two children, Laszlo and Asha.